By

## Nekisha Pickney and Noah Rattler

### Illustrated By Thaddeus Lavalais

# Dedications

## Noah's Dedication:

*Outside of my friends and family, the people who helped make me, I would like to dedicate this book to Mrs. Bridgewater, Mrs. Singleton and Mrs. Maura. These women took responsibility for the molding of generations of young minds. If you find a copy of this book, just know that I was listening.*

## Nekisha's Dedication:

*I dedicate this book to those that I am fortunate enough to have in my life; my children, family and friends. Thank you for your daily encouragement, love and support. I have to especially thank Noah for allowing me to be a part of telling his story; one that I am sure will touch the hearts and minds of many.*

# Friends of Noah's Walk
## Sponsorship Page

**Blueprint Improvement Group (BIG)**
http://www.think-b-i-g.com/

**Organizing Lifestyles**
http://www.organizinglifestyles.net/

**YBTurner Social Media Services**
www.YBTurner.com

Today's civics lesson is about how one person can make a difference.

This book is about Noah Rattler, a community activist who walked 1,800 miles from Houston, Texas all the way to Los Angeles, California, to raise awareness about homelessness.

When Noah was a little boy
he wanted to save the world...
Or at least make it a better place.

One day, Noah realized that there was a very big problem with homelessness in the United States of America! There are a lot of people, including children and their parents, who do not have a place to live, or have any food or water. Noah cared about solving this problem and took responsibility to help. So, Noah made a big decision! He would walk from city to city and state to state, all the while, telling others about the homeless and asking them to become involved to help the homeless, too.

## Now, let's accompany Noah on his walk...

Noah began his journey on March 24, 2007. After saying good-bye to lots of friends and family, he took his first steps with Jason, one of his best friends.

Although Jason only walked with Noah for the first two days, Noah realized that it helps to start a long journey with a good friend.

NOAH!

NOAH!

NOAH!

Jason Luckett
Educator

Laurence Payne
President & CEO,
SEARCH Project

Sheila Jackson Lee
U.S. Representative

4

Noah walked and walked. Twenty miles a day! He walked through the Piney Woods of East Texas, stopping at the support vehicle when he needed to eat, rest or sleep.

After walking for two weeks and 239 miles, Noah arrived in Dallas, Texas, where he was met by his new support team, Jari and her dog named Princess, a Toy Poodle.

6

Noah's mission required the help of many people to set up interviews with television stations, newspapers and radio stations. Noah also visited the places where homeless people stay, and talked to the people in the cities who helped them. These organizations and people are known as "homeless service providers." In the Dallas/Fort Worth area, Noah's friend Terrance sprang into action by planning these activities!

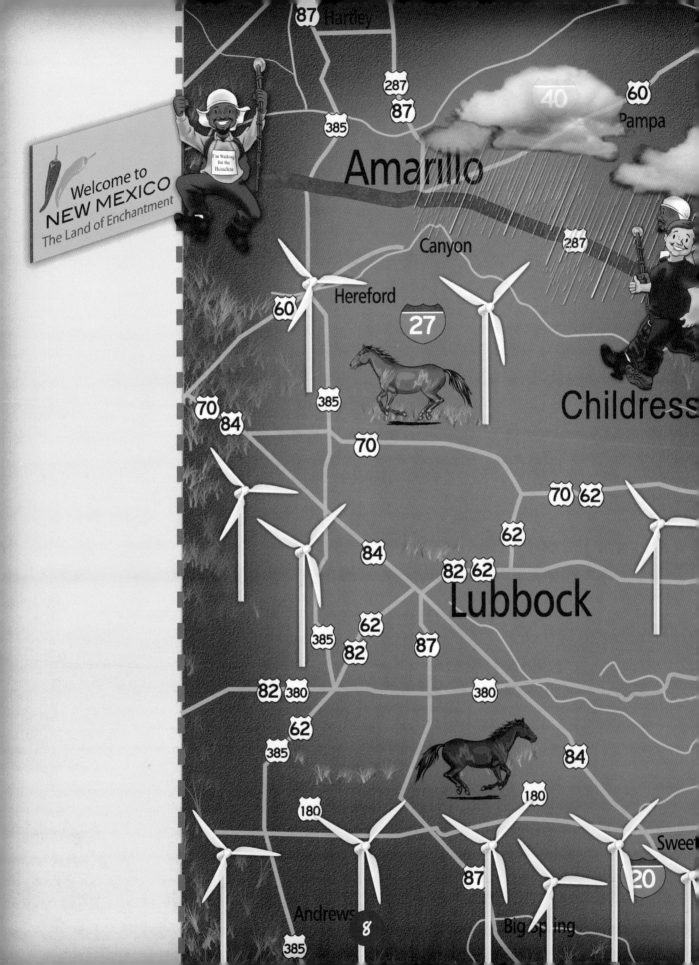

Over the next month Noah walked. Through April showers and May flowers, he walked, visiting organizations, speaking with the media, and spreading awareness however he could. Noah joined forces with his old friend Jabari in Wichita Falls, and his new friend Kim in Childress. 680 Miles later, he made it to the New Mexico Border. He had walked further than he had ever walked before, and he still had 2/3 of his journey ahead of him.

After crossing the border, Noah noticed something different about the tall grass he now had to walk through. There were snakes EVERYWHERE!!!

Whip snakes! Garter snakes! Bull snakes! Every ten steps, he would see another one. As a matter of fact, he almost stepped on a deadly Rattlesnake early one morning.

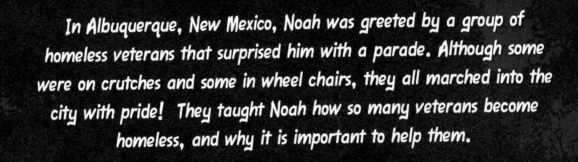

In Albuquerque, New Mexico, Noah was greeted by a group of homeless veterans that surprised him with a parade. Although some were on crutches and some in wheel chairs, they all marched into the city with pride! They taught Noah how so many veterans become homeless, and why it is important to help them.

After spending one week with the veterans, Noah headed west and into the Navajo Indian Reservation. There, he teamed up with his old friend Michael, who introduced Noah to Navajo Culture and life on the reservation. They also discussed poverty, homelessness and community activism in their communities.

As he continued west, Noah entered Arizona, known as the "Grand Canyon State." In Holbrook, Arizona, he learned more about the lives of the fastest growing group of homeless people, which are mothers and their children. He thought a lot about this as he walked through The Petrified Forest and The Painted Desert.

Noah thought and thought, as he walked all the way to the edge of the Grand Canyon.  It was 100 days later! Noah was 1,300 miles away from home. The Grand Canyon is really high too! 8,000 feet high, to be exact!

As Noah continued his journey, he moved deeper and deeper into the desert. Every step he took made the journey harder because the pain in his feet grew with each step, and each day was hotter than the one before it.

The day Noah walked into California, things were really hard! The sunlight in the Mojave Desert National Preserve was so intense that it felt heavy on his shoulders, like he was carrying the Sun itself! Because Noah had walked so far, the pain in his feet was bad enough to make him want to quit.

Noah could not quit because he made a commitment to himself and his community to see this walk through to the end. This commitment helped him push through the pain and heat, to walk further and faster than ever before.

WALKING FOR THE HOMELESS

The further he walked, the faster he approached the end of his journey. As he entered Los Angeles County, he was joined by two good friends John and Kisha, who walked with him as a show of support in the final days of his journey. As they passed through Los Angeles, he thought about the thousands of people that were homeless in this city, and all across the United States. This made him realize that his accomplishment was not enough, and more needed to be done.

Before he knew it, Noah found himself staring at the Pacific Ocean. Before a gathering crowd, with one foot in front of the other, Noah took the final steps of his journey. On August 4, 2007, after 134 days and 3,168,000 steps, Noah's walk came to an end. Noah stood in the Pacific Ocean, smiling, with his arms open wide! Mission Accomplished!

23

Well, what do you think, children?

Mrs. Jackson, can we help the homeless?

I like the story Mrs. Jackson. Noah was very brave... I think I will walk to the North Pole one day...

That's very good Carlos, and very brave of you. Yes, Kim?

Well, I am glad you asked Kim. That is your next homework assignment.

AWW!!

Each of you will need to find other examples of people helping the homeless, and come up with a plan that we can implement as a class. Noah made a difference by doing something very difficult in order to bring attention to the struggles of millions of men, women and children across this country.

He was one person. Imagine what we can accomplish as a class. Think about that on your way home today.

Class dismissed.

24

# Glossary

<u>Activist</u> - Someone who believes in or practices trying to make social or political changes through action.

<u>Awareness</u> - Having knowledge or a perception of a situation or fact.

<u>Civics</u> - The study of the rights and duties of citizenship.

<u>Commitment</u> - Being dedicated to a cause or activity.

<u>Culture</u> - The sum of the language, customs, beliefs, and art considered to denote a particular group of people.

<u>Inhabitants</u> - People that permanently live in a place; residents.

<u>Implement</u> - To carry out or put into effect.

<u>Military</u> - The armed forces. In the United States, the military is comprised of the Army, Navy, Marine Corps, Air Force and the U.S. Coast Guard.

<u>Veteran</u> - People who served in the military in the United States  U.S. Army, Navy, Marine Corps, Air Force, and Coast Guard  during times of war or peace.

<u>Population</u> - All the inhabitants of a particular town, area, or country.

# Animals of the Walk

White Tailed Deer

 Kit Fox

Quarter Horse

Coyote

Beef Cow

Mountain Lion

Prong Horn Buck

Crow

Rattlesnake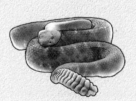

Red Tailed Hawk

Peccary

Golden Eagle

Road Runner

California Condor

# Photos from Noah's Walk

Noah helps to feed the homeless in Dallas-Fort Worth

Noah in Santa Rosa on his way to the Flying C Ranch

At the Grand Canyon with support team member Jari

Noah communes with the horses on his way from
Amarillo, Texas to Tucumari, New Mexico

Noah at the end of his journey at Santa Monica Beach in California